Unbottled

Olivia Dawson

Maytree Press 2022

Published 2022 by Maytree Press

www.maytreepress.co.uk

ISBN: 978-1-913508-30-2

A CIP catalogue record of this book is available from the British Library.

Cover image: Sakura by Samantha Read

Maytree 040

Printed in the UK

Acknowledgements

Versions of some of these poems have previously appeared in *Eye Flash Poetry* and *Iamb-poetry seen and heard.*

I owe very special thanks to my half-aunt Elisabeth Steen Woodroffe, who has generously shared many stories, documents, and photographs.

Huge thanks to Jean White, my newly found cousin, who has been so welcoming, interested, and immensely generous, with her sharing of family photographs and memories.

I am very grateful to my mentor Rebecca Goss, who inspires me to reach beyond my comfort zone and makes anything seem possible.

Thank you to Nicole Gunn, a brilliant genealogist, (findingjohnandjane.com) who swiftly put the final pieces of the puzzle into place.

Thanks are due to The Poetry School for their wonderful courses and tutors, and to the Lisbon Stanza for their insightful responses to my poems and their warm friendship.

All love and thanks to my daughter Leonora Lockhart, who travelled with me on this adventure into our DNA, came with me on investigative expeditions, and shared my excitement as we discovered family links.

As always, all love and thanks to my husband Bruce, and to my family, for their encouragement and, much relied on, humour.

i.m. Monica Marie-Therese
3/3/1920 – 23/11/ 2017

Contents:

Prologue

Spitting into Bottles

My mother's mother has a lover
my mother's mother's lover is a puzzle
my mother's mother leaves my mother
in a Home for awkward silences.

A mother-to-no-one loves
my mother's dimples, takes my mother in
feeds her fresh baked cinnamon swirls
gives her a father-figure who whistles

but my mother searches and searches
finds her blood mother who tells her nothing
my mother searches and searches
finds half-of-a-much-younger-sister

who isn't silenced. My mother's half-
of-a-much-younger-sister doesn't know
there's another half, she doesn't know a thing.
My mother's other half, half looks

like me and my father wobbles
when he spots our sameness, warns me
off boys. I spit into a bottle to find
my mother's mother's runaway lover

I spit into another bottle to find the mother
of my mother's mother's lover, I want to discover
why I'm not blessed with long slim legs
and a thigh gap like no other.

Part 1: Home for Awkward Silences

Untitled

(Age:1y 3m. Position in Institution: Inmate)

I've a photo of a row of toddlers
all with glossy nameless faces

from a story of a lost village
once a haven for untimely babies,

the littlest child unsettles me
the way pebbles disturb smooth water.

Once Upon a Time once upon a time

near Deepdene Bridge over the river Mole
a lonely baby girl grew plump on rosehips.
One evening a solitary woman strolled past

bewitched by the girl's tangle of golden curls.
She scooped her up and carried her home carefully
as a brown paper bag of freshly laid eggs.

The little girl had nearly all she could wish for
in her new home with its four walls, lattice windows,
floors skiddy with beeswax. The lady knitted all day,

the girl had lacy fingertips, moss stitch shoes,
a rose stitch hairbrush for her rose stitch dolls.
On Sundays the lady washed the girl's curls

and trimmed her ringlets when they grew too wild,
saving the softest to plump up her intarsia cushions.
The girl was left to play alone all day and felt

something was missing. She looked for it everywhere:
struggled to reach the back of the wardrobe, flipped
through pages of *The Velveteen Rabbit*, unzipped

heart-shaped pillows to comb through fluffy fibres.
One autumn day, a whistling boy foraging
for his fill of chanterelles in Slipshatch Wood

8

surprised the-girl-with-the-golden-curls,
who, prowling around him like a cat, sensed
this boy was her missing part. She threw him

her torn heart unravelled from her sleeve,
but still felt hollow inside - she fretted her DNA
might display unlovable strands of angora goat.

Untruth

After six months your mother tries
to visit you but is told you've been chosen

by another mother, so she leaves
for an adventure in Venezuela,

believes she's too late to reclaim you,
while you tumble through your toddler years

waiting to be selected, spruced up for visitors
like a pre-loved *Special Occasions* dress on Etsy.

Adopted

They wanted to refashion you as *Marie*
after some French cousin but she died young
by misadventure. At eighteen you shrug
on *Marie* for fun, shoulder her sins,

Bless me Father I am going to die, the priest
cracks his knuckles in a slow staccato.
Marie would have bolted – you bolt.
Marie would have lifted a Kit Kat from the kiosk,

you lift two, chase crumbs around your lips
with your tongue. You drift to *Urgence,* sign *Marie*
with a smiley, tell them you are going to die,
but they worry about your fiscal number,

a security guard with a single eyebrow
says he needs *Nom Complet* for your Death Certificate,
calls you *une jeune fille dangereuse.* On impulse
you dash into traffic, adopt your new persona.

Finding the Lost Village i
(Erasure poem - source M M-T's diary, June 1962)

summer

somewhere

lane

farm   eyeing

desolation

overgrown

dark

forgotten

years   here

Unforgetting
(After Leonora Lockhart 'UnderStory' in slip cast porcelain, 2019)

                pale
    porcelain

           cup

              *

       from memory
               at tipping point
erased
        ghost
                    of your hand
           knows
          the chipped rim
    your   lips   unforget

              *

faded
        balanced
      indigo flowers and sprigs
   invoke   old roses
the weight of the cup
   the way your finger   curves
senses the handle
      scarred   table

              *

Finding the Lost Village ii
13ᵗʰ September 2021 - 51°11'28.6"N 0°12'09.4"W

Thatched roofs with tall brick chimneys
appear/disappear/appear/disappear,

camouflaged by bitter yew threaded
through with ripening blackberries.

The muddy lane funnels with rain,
I trespass across a scarred lawn, pause

under a stucco dove with clipped wings
pinioned over an arched doorway,

I squelch through a sting of nettles, slip
on moss-covered tiles where children once prayed,

kneel where my mother knelt on dinted knees
while she waited for someone to love her.

Part 2: My Mother's Mother

Possible Point of Departure

Her eyes throw him off-kilter
followed by the insides of her wrists

she's lightly touched with *Shalimar.*
She scarecrows her arms east and west

feels him smooth the cool skin
in the crook of her elbow,

coaxes him to find her waypoint
where butterflies stir beneath

the surface. He's drawn
by a magnetic pull as she eases

her legs apart, knees quivering
like feather grass, feet balanced

on scrappy sand, testing
the best way forward.

Strangers

(Erasure poem - source M M-T's diary, April 1963)

            a stranger

    stared   silently

eyes   brighter

                        resemblance

    silence

        I am

          I am

                mother

                    numbed

    superficial

          small-talk

                  silence   tangible

                    separating

Tonibell Time

Home early from school
I find a half-familiar lady
In the kitchen with Mum.

They swing their heads
like synchronised dolls
and stare right through me.

Outside sounds the same
as yesterday, kids play tag
while the ice cream van

chimes its delicious tune
but Mum doesn't hug me,
flicks me like an irritant

then knits her fingers
in a mirror image
of the lady who announces:

I'm your gran. I have two
of those already but
from out of the corner

of my eye I see her foot
jiggle just like mine
which will drive Mum wild.

Mirror Image

They make it
look so easy
tapping
their clay
to centre it
on the wheel
smoothing
rough earth
into a curve
that turns &
meanders
under linked
fingers.

I sit
elbows-to-hips
centre
my self
throw
worked mud
watch it
wobble
& flop
lopsided
as the tilt
of their lips.

Tell Me

(Erasure poem – source M M-T's diary, May 1963)

                                   trace

          tell me   father

             true

         war

      Shock
baby

                    no help

    no trace

        posed   false name

                 tears

Mismatch

Maybe they never fitted together
unlike my jigsaw puzzle
of the Leaning Tower of Pisa,
a complex design of columns
and arches, shock orange
in the setting sun,
with a slice of celestial
blue, where the *campanile,*
(bells stifled), pulls away
from the grey *cattedrale.*
Shored up, the tower strains
at flawed foundations,
clings to uncertain ground
with blind faith. One day
pieces will concertina,
crush anyone struggling
to escape unbroken.

How to Cut and Fit your Sweetheart

Don't shape armholes too close,
avoid chafing and sweat stains,
leave space to turn cartwheels

with ease. Match openings
to sleeves with balance marks
meticulously pinned. Track

the true bust-line, enhance
rosebud breasts with crafty darts
nipped and tucked to the best

advantage. Manipulate seams,
leave no baggy fabric, lead the eye
to a wedding ring waist.

If it's tricky to breathe
keep her intake shallow, until she
is trimmed to your perfect fit.

Alternative Choices

She scrawls lists of *moments/ mistakes/ triumphs*
she *enjoys/ regrets/ forgets,* like the boy
she *fancied/ abandoned/ believed,* his name
scribbled as a *red-herring/ memo/ joke* on a yellow stickie,
the daughter she might have *lost/ kept/ loved,*
the prayer she can't get straight, muddling *fruit/ womb,*
her stash *of disappointments/ Black Magic/ lipstick*
lingering under a mattress, *Twister/ revenge/ keep fit*
in the lounge, *arms/ smoke/ spittle* swirling every which way.
She clings to the daily *visitor/ crossword/ headache*
to avoid *rejection/ hope/ discovery* dodges the clues,
holds *answers/ memories/ secrets* to the light
wondering who fills them in and when you tell her
you *forgive/ understand/ need* her, she asks:
*How **many** boys/ babies/ lies?*

Part 3: My Mother's Mother's Lover

Alternative Pathways

('A gene is ... more like a story ... ', Sam Kean)

I resemble a fluke   I want to resemble my mother
I have hazel eyes   we resemble our patterns
my brother has blue eyes   like an underwater volcano
resembles my mother   her innate trait
we resemble our patterns   the colour of his eyes
I want to resemble my mother   resembles someone else
with her bubble of a laugh   my laugh my mother's
like an underwater volcano   someone laughs like a giant
my brother doesn't laugh   we erupt into bubbles
he resembles a fluke   I have hazel eyes
my laugh my mother's   I resemble a fluke
my daughter's laugh   with his bubble of a laugh
resembles a bubble   we dive to catch
her innate trait   my daughter's laugh
like my mother's mother   resembles my mother
someone laughs like a giant   resembles a bubble
resembles someone else   my brother has blue eyes
we dive to catch   like my mother's mother
the colour of his eyes   she resembles a fluke
we erupt into bubbles   my brother doesn't laugh

Cosmetologist Creates Shampoo Infused with Sound

It's hard to trap snuffles of a baby's breath,
the sssh of foam at low tide or the exhausted sigh
of a heart when it breaks. I need silence, a sleight of hand,

butterfly nets, Blu Tack to catch elusive threads,
a freezer set to *hoar frost* until echoes split
ready to be grated and mixed with white peach.

Of course I make mistakes, the last batch picked up
the zing of a trampoline spring from over the garden wall,
but uncork this flask and listen to your story.

Ballerina on a Bucking Bronco

There's a whisper my unnamed grandfather
gifted migraines to my daughter. Rumour says
he's from Texas, with eyes clear as the Chihuahuan night sky,

rumour says he's a storyteller, but my sister rides horses
like an acrobat, my brother enjoys stalking, sneaks
on his belly, cap sprigged with purple heather,
I'm a ballerina, arms lifted to the stars like a cartoon cactus.

Rumour says my grandfather poses in an arabesque
on a bucking bronco while he shoots at tin cans,
a Stetson on his head for protection from the sun,
recoiling when he fires his rifle to bring down his targets
one by one by one.

Unbottled

('Once discoveries are made, we can't undo them.' Ancestry.com)

A ribbon of spittle matches me
with the untold gift of one hundred & six Texans,
    five close cousins, a family name

that's unfamiliar. They lead me
    to a leafy tree, reach distinctive fingers,
release an *L* tethered to seven other letters

    strung together like festive bunting
vibrant with my blood relations,
    linking me to Blaze, Dallas, Jean,

Sandra, Junior, Cheryl, Rob, Karen,
    Anna, James, Clint, Frank, Denver & Cal,
who I need to unravel before they shy

    from the double twist of mother & daughter,
& shuffle all ties, masking the scent
    of my mother's mother's lover.

Traits Report

I am average, with a 50/50 chance of most things,
my hair is likely to be straight or wavy, my thighs

dimpled with bitterness, possibly I have an aversion
to ability and fear probably bites me more often than others.

I'm predicted to have mosquito pitch, a dislike
of speaking sounds, an average chance of wet earwax,

perhaps higher odds than most of waking at 7.04 a.m.
with a possible detachment from good taste.

I'm likely to have a little freckling, a 73% chance
of my big toe being sweeter than my asparagus odour,

but I have fewer chewing variants than 58% of my ancestors,
which makes me 8% more (or is it less?) special.

On the estimated date of conception

(Four of the boys are already under France's skies and the other two are ready for the call overseas.
- Leslie's Weekly – 1918)

one brother goes home in daylight, one brother is 5' 10"
tall, one has a scar, one wears a wedding ring. One brother
studies Civic Liability, a moonlight before, or after, the
estimated date of conception. One brother is demobbed,
one recovers from a fever in Bushy Park, one is a smoker,
one is taller than the others, one votes for the Democrats,
one has blue eyes, one is a Methodist. One brother sails
from Brest on 14th July 1919, a month after the estimated
date of conception, one reveals diamond-patterned socks,
one is a mechanic, one returns to England before the
estimated date of conception, one has hazel eyes, one stays
at the YMCA, one has a shiny tie painted with a covered
wagon, one is my mother's mother's lover.

Finding Robert

Marlin-Falls
brothers *Cactus* single
WW1 graduated slim voter
Dieppe California census birth

traits		school
census		life
studied		church
obituary		probate
register		*Leslie's Weekly*
characteristics		family
slender		census
survived	Robert	Texas
census		ring finger
match		scar
London		draft
Brest		6' 1/4" tall
demobbed		Santa Fe
Law		died

veteran university smoker DNA
wife couple census Fort-Worth
Rancho cousins ancestors
spittle certificate
find-a-grave

Alternative Scenarios

For J.W.

Today I see the first photo
I've ever seen of Robert,

his face so familiar I long to drop
into the picture, inhale the linger

from his cigarette, smooth his suit
of linen sunshine with my fingers.

Did he know that you existed,
that you flew to Texas in the 60s,

cradling a name – not listed –
tricked to a hometown – misdirected –

as if he'd chosen to deflect you
or as if some clown had juggled

with your lives – your mother
despatched to the seaside

to paint cowslips on teacups,
and you – spirited away

through a maze of smoke and mirrors.
I can't decide what narrative

you might have adopted
as your fiction.

Epilogue

Just this once

I want to see my grandparents together:

'Jeanne & Robert'

Notes

Untitled (P.7) *'Age:1y 3m. Position in Institution: Inmate':* from the 1921 Census of England and Wales, the Babies Haven, Duxhurst.

The *'photo'* is from *'Duxhurst – Surrey's Lost Village'* by Ros Black, (Arbe Publications, 2011), p.51 with the caption On The Wagon and attributed to Wasted Wealth a booklet by Lady Henry Somerset, 1917.

Once Upon a Time (P.8) *The Velveteen Rabbit* by Margery Williams (George H. Doran Company, 1922)

Tonibell Time (P.17) The iconic Tonibell ice cream vans have been selling Tonibell ice cream since the 1960s in the UK. The vans have recognisable chimes that announce their arrival in a neighbourhood, often at the time children are coming out of school.

Alternative Pathways (P.23) *'A gene is … more like a story … 'from 'The Violinist's Thumb: And Other Lost Tales of Love, War, and Genius, as Written by Our Genetic Code'* by Sam Kean (Little, Brown, 2012).

Traits Report (P.27) Found poem – source text Olivia Dawson's *23andMe* DNA Traits Report.

About the Author

Olivia Dawson, originally from London, has also lived in France and Brazil. She divides her time between London, and the Sintra Hills near Lisbon, and is the Poetry Society Stanza rep for the Lisbon area. Recent poems have been published in *14 Magazine, Eye Flash Poetry, Iamb - poetry seen and heard, Alchemy Spoon, Magma, Poetry Birmingham Literary Journal, Time & Tide (Arachne Press) Coast to Coast to Coast, The Poetry Village, ROAM 1* of The University of Lisbon Centre for English Studies. She has been longlisted for the National Poetry Competition, shortlisted for Paper Swans Press Pamphlet Competition, and shortlisted for Poetry on the Lake Competition. Her debut pamphlet *Unfolded* was published by Maytree Press in 2020 and *Unbottled* is her second pamphlet.